WALTER·CRANE

WALTER·CRANE
·AS·A·BOOK·
·ILLUSTRATOR·

RODNEY·K·ENGEN

·ACADEMY·EDITIONS·LONDON·
·ST·MARTIN'S·PRESS·NEW·YORK·

·ACKNOWLEDGEMENTS·

For permission to photograph the works of Walter Crane, I wish to thank the Library and Print Department of the Victoria and Albert Museum and the Photo Archive of the Witt Library. I also wish to acknowledge the assistance of the staff of the British Museum; the William Morris Museum, Walthamstow; Frederick Leighton House, Holland Park; the Ashmolean Museum, Oxford and the Fitzwilliam Museum, Cambridge. In addition, the research assistance of Margaret Challen and personal guidance of Trebbe Johnson were much appreciated.

FRONTISPIECE
Walter Crane by Fred Hollyer

FACING PAGE ILLUSTRATIONS
(above) Decorative book heading, 1887
(below) Illuminated letter 'A' from a design entitled *Night*, 1893

First published in Great Britain in 1975 by
Academy Editions   7 Holland Street, London, W8
Cloth SBN 85670 155 6   Paper SBN 85670 170 X
Copyright © Academy Editions 1975. All rights reserved
First Published in the U.S.A. in 1975 by St Martin's Press Inc.
175 Fifth Avenue, New York, N.Y. 10010
Library of Congress Catalog Card Number 73-91330
Printed and bound in Great Britain at Burgess and Son (Abingdon) Ltd

· INTRODUCTION ·

book may be the home of both thought and vision. Speaking figuratively, in regard to book decoration, some are content with a rough shanty in the woods, and care only to get as close to nature, in her more superficial aspects, as they can. Others would surround their house with a garden indeed, but they demand something like an architectural plan. They would look at the Frontispiece like a façade; they would take hospitable encouragement from the title page as from a friendly inscription over the porch; they would hang a votive wreath in dedication, and so pass on into the hall of welcome, take the author by the hand and be led by him and his artist from room to room, as page after page is turned, fairly decked and adorned with picture, and ornament, and device; and perhaps finding it a dwelling after his desire, the guest is content to rest in the single nook in the firelight of the spirit of the author or the play of fancy of the artist; and, weaving dreams in the changing lights and shadows to forget life's rough way and the tempestuous world outside' (*Of the Decorative Illustration of Books Old and New*, 1896).

Walter Crane's childhood was filled with a great variety of artistic influences. Born in 1845, just six years before the Great Exhibition which was to herald Victorian ingenuity and eclectic taste in the decorative arts, Crane could remember the accounts of his parents who had visited the Exhibition. His father was a lithographer and portrait artist who with his three brothers had worked in Chester, drawing and publishing such works as *The History of the Pig and Miss Crane*. Thomas Crane later became Secretary and Treasurer of the Liverpool Academy of Art.

As a boy, Crane worked in his father's studio sketching the hands and faces of his father's portrait commissions. He studied the engraved illustrations of John Gilbert in the *Illustrated London News*, often colouring in these fine-lined drawings. Gilbert was a major influence upon the popular illustration of the time and an important model for Crane's early works (*Multiplication Table in Verse*, page 28). Crane was also attracted by the powerful sixteenth-century German woodcuts published at this time in the *Art Journal*.

When he moved to London in 1857 Crane continued his drawing practice while working as an engraver's apprentice to W. J. Linton, a noted master engraver, writer, poet and champion of political freedom. Linton recognized Crane's skill as an inventive designer and gave him work specifically to develop this talent. John Ruskin had visited Linton's business and admired

Crane's drawings to Tennyson's *Lady of Shalott*, a popular subject also drawn by Rossetti in the contemporary Pre-Raphaelite style. Linton sent Crane to make studies of animals at the Zoological Gardens for a projected natural history volume and here Crane learned the importance of spontaneous line for the recording of an object in time. These animal studies were often modelled after the works of Sir Edwin Landseer, the noted painter recognized by the Queen, both for his studies of dogs and as the sculptor of the lions in Trafalgar Square (see *Cock Robin*, page 25). Crane's experience with Linton's firm varied from drawing iron bedsteads for mail-order catalogues, and medical dissection diagrams, to engraving biblical and book illustrations and sketching aspects of court cases for the magazine *News of the World*.

Crane eventually left the Linton firm in 1862 to begin illustrating independently. That same year he was commissioned to illustrate J. R. Wise's *The New Forest, its History and Scenery*, a book describing the woodland areas which the author and Crane himself had explored on foot. Crane's engraved vignettes of different aspects of the landscape soon gained him the reputation of being a child prodigy, which he resented. Although he was only seventeen at the time, he considered himself a professional illustrator.

The following year Edmund Evans, a watercolour artist and businessman who was interested in producing more tastefully coloured children's books, commissioned Crane to complete a set of designs for a projected book series. He believed that the quality of paper picture books could be greatly improved and still sold for sixpence 'if printed in sufficient quantity'. This was the period of greater mechanization in publishing, which was often used as an excuse to neglect artistic design. Publishers at first protested to Evans that the raw, vulgar and coarse designs then being produced appealed to a larger public and therefore paid better. However, Crane's tasteful designs were printed by Evans for the publisher Frederick Warne in a yellow-bound *Sixpenny Toybook* series. The yellow cover was Evans' idea; he considered it would be far more practical to use pale yellow enamelled paper covers instead of the easily soiled white cover of the Victorian popular literature. The concept was soon adopted for most cheap railway novels, then called 'mustard plaisters'. *Cock Robin, Dame Trot and her Comical Cat* and *The House that Jack Built* were books Crane illustrated for Warne at this time.

George Routledge soon took advantage of the success of the *Sixpenny Toybooks* published by Warne and issued his own series, which Crane began designing in 1867, and which eventually became the most popular children's books of the day. These early designs were influenced by Crane's study of some Japanese prints shown him by a naval friend. He wrote: 'Their treatment, in definite block outline and flat, brilliant, as well as delicate colours, struck me at once and I endeavoured to apply these methods to the modern fanciful and humorous subjects of children's toybooks and the methods of wood-engraving and machine-printing' (*An Artist's Reminiscences*). The Routledge *Sixpenny* and *Shilling Toybooks* were to include such titles as *The Old Courtier* (page 27), *Multiplication Table in Verse* (page 28), *Grammar in Rhyme* and *Annie and Jack in London* (pages 29–30). *This little Pig went to Market* (page 34), and *The Fairy Ship* (page 33) showed a distinct flattening of forms and elaborate line typical of Japanese prints. Crane continued: 'About 1869–70 they (picture books) began to show something like a distinctive treatment and style, as I endeavoured to adapt them more both to the conceptions of children and to the conditions of colour-printing' (*An Artist's Reminiscences*).

Crane married in 1871 and visited Rome, where he completed several more children's books. The demand for new books was now limited to two books per year as Crane was also designing room interiors, friezes and tapestries with his contemporaries William Morris, Burne-Jones and Philip Webb. While in Rome he developed a sketch-like immediacy in line drawings and watercolours by executing a drawing in black and white on card and sending it to Evans, who photographed it and then had the drawing engraved, while the proofs were sent back to Crane for colouring. This new method of working replaced the tedious practice of drawing directly

Walter Crane's studio at Shepherd's Bush

on the block for the engraver to follow and encouraged a more spontaneous drawing style. The success of Crane's colour books was marked by Routledge re-issuing in 1874 a bound set of *Sixpenny Toybooks* entitled *Walter Crane's Picturebook*.

Crane moved to Wood Lane, Shepherd's Bush (page 3) and there completed in 1875 a new series of toybooks, including *Aladdin* (page 62), *The Yellow Dwarf* (page 57), *Beauty and the Beast* (pages 52–55), *Princess Belle Etoile* (page 56) and *Goody Two Shoes* (pages 58–59). All the drawings for these books were done at a modest cost, as Crane sold the drawings directly to the publishers. Since engraving and printing were the costliest aspect of production, as many as 50,000 books were necessary to make the book series profitable. Unlike many of his contemporaries such as Kate Greenaway and Randolph Caldecott, Crane did not receive royalties for his designs, but commented: 'However, if they did not bring in much money, I had my fun out of them, as in designing. I was in the habit of putting in all sorts of subsidiary detail that interested me, and often made them the vehicle for my ideas in furniture and decoration' (*An Artist's Reminiscences*).

Crane did receive commissions for decorative work as a result of the success of his book illustrations, such as the friezes which he designed for the home of Mr Lee of Worcester, using the drawings in his *Aesop's Fables* for patterns. Also important is the interior work done by Crane in 1880 for Alexander Ionides' House at 1 Holland Park. And in 1875 he was commissioned by Messrs Jeffreys and Company, the printers of William Morris wallpapers, to design a series of wallpapers for the nursery based upon his successful book designs. The designs were divided into three columns by a narrow border and the outlines of faces were formed by brass wire, which limited subtle detail but contributed to the decorative effect of the paper. This work was popular enough to be copied by rival firms (page 4).

Wallpaper design, 1876

In 1874, Crane began illustrating the stories of Mrs Molesworth (1839–1911), a woman who completed over one hundred books for adults and children. The child-like grammar and moralizing tones of her work were often criticized for their innovation. *Tell me a Story* was the first of sixteen of these books illustrated by Crane, which included *The Rectory Children*, 1889 (page 5) and ended with *The Children of the Castle* in 1890 (pages 81–82).

Crane's designs for the Routledge *Toybook* series ended with *The Sleeping Beauty in the Wood*, 1876. He then returned to work with Edmund Evans on a different type of children's book, which was to incorporate music with illustrations. *The Baby's Opera*, 1877 (pages 63–64) was a five-shilling children's book, rejected by the book trade for its advanced design, but accepted by the public, who demanded a printing of over 40,000 copies. Crane followed its success with a sequel, *The Baby's Bouquet*, 1878 (Plate VII), which included German, French and English songs translated by Crane's sister Lucy.

Children's education was to play an important part in Crane's designs. In 1884 he joined with J. M. D. Meiklejohn, Professor of Education and Language at St Andrews University to produce *The Golden Primer*, the text and illustrations of which were designed to teach children words by associating them with pictures. 'Teach only words, teach them as wholes! Never mention the name of a letter unless the child demands it', the endpapers of the book warned the reader. Crane was to continue this interest with designs for Miss Nellie Dale's *The Walter Crane Reader*, 1899. Miss Dale was pioneering a system of teaching children to read through the use of sounds and letters which were allotted colours for identification. It was followed by *The Dale Readers Book II* in 1907.

Oscar Wilde was also a friend and associate of Crane during the time Wilde was editor of *Woman's World*, an illustrated journal of women's fashion and literature. Wilde in fact published a Crane drawing in the magazine alongside a poem written by Beatrice, Crane's younger daughter. Wilde also reviewed Crane's book *Flora's Feast* in his magazine. In 1888, Crane and George P. J. Hood were commissioned by Wilde to illustrate an edition of Wilde's stories for children *The Happy Prince* (pages 79–80) for which Crane contributed three full-page illustrations.

As the socialist movement gained strength in England, Crane became involved in politics. His association with William Morris and George Bernard Shaw prompted him to join the Socialist League in 1883 and he was persuaded to contribute a weekly cartoon to various socialist periodicals such as *Justice* and *The Commonweal*, and to lecture before meetings of Shaw's Fabian Society which were attended by such notables as Oscar Wilde and Yeats. Crane's illustrations for children, subject to these influences, became more and more complex, and the range of his audiences grew wider. *Echoes of Hellas* (pages 77–78), the Kelmscott edition of *The Glittering Plain* (page 86), illustrations for Spenser's *Faerie Queen* (pages 88–89), *Cartoons for the Cause* (pages 95–96), Shakespeare's *Two Gentlemen of Verona* (page 90), *The Merry Wives of Windsor* (page 91) and *A Flower Wedding* used themes with mythological or social symbolism which appealed to a more adult reader.

Crane was a primary figure in the movement to re-establish the importance of the craftsman in English society. He was the first president of the Arts Workers' Guild in 1884, later President

Title page to *The Rectory Children* by Mrs Molesworth, 1889

of the Arts and Crafts Society (1888–90 and 1895–1915), and Director of Design at Manchester School of Art, 1893–96). As Principal of the Royal College of Art (1896–99), Crane wrote and lectured concerning the need for good design, craftsmanship and standards of taste in an England of eclectic Victorian taste. His aesthetic theories were published as collected essays in *The Bases of Design*, 1898, and in such guides for students as *Of the Decorative Illustration of Books Old and New*, 1896, and *Line and Form*, 1900.

In addition to illustration, interior design and decorative friezes, Crane also painted rather academic canvases; his first exhibition was held at the Royal Academy in 1862 when he was seventeen. He wrote poetry and illustrated his poems: *The Sirens Three*, 1886 (pages 72–74) reveals the strong influence of *The Rubá'iyát of Omar Khayyám*.

Crane died in 1915, a major figure in the English popular and decorative arts of the nineteenth century. As one of the 'Academics of the Nursery', he helped, through his books for children, to further the development of book illustration for the education and pleasure of children both in England and abroad.

Crane's boyhood during the Victorian age left a distinct influence upon his later children's illustrations. This was the period when schoolmasters favoured the classical style of beauty which they felt to be epitomized in the arts of the Ancient Greeks. Such a style was to create a distinct attitude in the Victorian mind, turning the rising middle-class youth of Britain into 'strong and upright aristocrats with an artificial emphasis upon masculine perfection and strength'. Walter Pater and Oscar Wilde wrote of the importance of a life of style, based upon an established standard of good taste, which Wilde called the 'New Hellenism'. These Aesthetes, as they were called, believed that the Victorians lacked such a standard of tasteful selection and appreciation of everyday objects, and favoured those mass-produced objects which borrowed from a motley of styles, from eighteenth-century French flamboyance to the purity of Greek line. Crane assessed the situation thus: 'A reaction had begun against the heavy and vulgar taste borrowed from the French Empire which had for twenty years or more dominated Victorian taste in English house decoration and furniture, and many artists were making efforts under new influences in more sincere and refined directions. The increased study of Gothic architecture, the writings of John Ruskin, the study of the Middle Ages, the study of Greek and Italian art, and the influence of the collection at South Kensington must have counted as factors in the new movement which reflected in individual hands many of these different influences and sources of inspiration' (*An Artist's Reminiscences*).

Study from Crane's book *Line and Form*, 1900

Lewis Day, writer for the Arts and Crafts Movement, and author of various design handbooks for the craftsmen of the day, including *Application of Ornament or Some Principles of Everyday Art*, wrote that this borrowing of the styles of the past by craftsmen was necessary, since England did not have a marked national style. He believed such revivals to be beneficial, since modern travel and processes of mechanical reproduction had been able to broaden the standards of good taste. In fact a few decorative artists did manage to maintain a distinctive individual style, although their work was open to interpretation as borrowings from medieval, Japanese, Moresque or Renaissance art. Walter Crane's work would have been placed in this category.

Industrialization did influence Crane's attitudes toward decoration and the role of the craftsman. At the same time as the splendours of the Crystal Palace were unveiled as triumphs of Victorian manufacture, English workers of the 1880s were living in the squalor and misery of an industrialized Dickensian world. Crane interpreted this increase in mechanized production as one of the factors encouraging the separation of artist and handicraftsman. 'Art must be produced for the people (or to sell to them) but it is no longer produced by the people', he argued. Due to the mechanization of the printing industry the number of books printed in England between 1828 and 1853 was increased from 842 to 2,330. Crane used an analogy inspired by children's stories to describe the problem of art and industry.

'Commerce, like the old woman in the nursery tale, stands at the stile (of an over-stocked market) with her obdurate pig (over-production) that refuses to move until the stick (of new demand) has been persuaded to bring its influence to bear...This little allegory from the nursery fits the situation exactly' (*An Artist's Reminiscences*).

As a result of those beliefs, Crane became involved with William Morris and Burne-Jones and their efforts to revive the importance of English craftsmanship, and personally concentrated on developing designs for mass-produced yet tasteful wallpapers and book illustrations.

'Every child, one might say every human being, takes in more through his eyes than his ears, and I think much more advantage might be taken of this fact' (*Of the Decorative Illustration of Books Old and New*). Crane was probably referring to the Victorian books for children which were designed to be read by a parent to his child, composed of concise line engravings in the style of John Gilbert, and with a distinct moralizing tone to the text, which the parent probably read beforehand to approve.

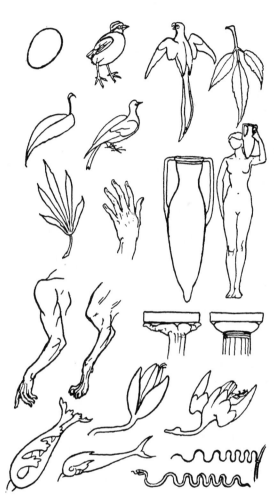

Study from Crane's book *Line and Form*, 1900

Up to this time children's books had been neglected by illustrators and writers. From the end of the eighteenth century 'books for the young' were peddled by street merchants, with crude woodcut designs or 'the penny plain and twopence coloured order' published by J. Lumsden and Sons, Glasgow, or J. Newbery, St Paul's Churchyard, London. The idea of well-designed fairy tales for educating children may have been initiated by the French treatise *The Education of Daughters*, 1687, written by Fénélon, Archbishop of Cambrai, in which he specified that books to teach children to enjoy reading should be cheerful fairy tales with fine illustrations, in gilt-edged volumes. However, this treatise could unfortunately apply only to the very rich families. An early attempt at such innovative book design was *The History of Goody Two Shoes*, published by J. Newbery in 1765, and written by an unknown author, believed to be Oliver Goldsmith. The original edition is now in the British Museum.

Austin Dobson was the first English bookseller to issue children's books as a major business venture. He sponsored such titles as *The Renowned History of Giles Gingerbread, Mrs Margery Two Shoes* and *Tommy Trip and his dog Joulen*. Such editions were coloured for printing by children in their teens who worked around a table, each with his watercolour and brush, a partly-coloured guide and a pile of printed uncoloured sheets. One child would paint the red, another the yellow, until the entire design was completed. However, in the early nineteenth century children's books remained of a moralistic and melancholy nature, with 'stilted and affected phrasing' and such titles as *The Child's Spiritual Treasury, The First Principles of Religion and the Existence of a Deity explained in a Series of Dialogues adapted to the Capacity of the Infant Mind*, or such grotesque topics as *A Child's Thoughts on Death*. It was not until the 1840s, when the *Home Treasury Series* was written by Sir Henry Cole and published by Joseph Cundall, that a conscious effort was made to produce a well-illustrated and well-designed children's storybook with leather covers and gilt-edged pages. *Little Red Riding Hood, Beauty and the Beast* and *Jack and the Beanstalk* were their first titles published in 1843, followed by *The Alphabet of Quadrupeds* in 1844, *Cinderella*, 1845, and *Tales from Spenser's Faerie Queen* and *The History of Reynard the Fox*, 1846. Among those producing illustrations for the firm were J. C. Horsley, T. Webster, R. Redgrave and J. Townsend. Most of the drawings were done in the style of vignettes and coloured by hand. Drawings of Renaissance maidens and Moorish interiors, as well as the similarity of the titles, prefigured the later designs of Walter Crane.

The technical aspects of book production were also undergoing change. Crane's *Toybooks* for Warne and Routledge were limited in colour scale to the red, blue and black of the engraver's block, so that the crudeness of the design was unavoidable. As the colour scale increased, areas of pink and emerald green were laid across faces and dresses in a somewhat reckless manner. But Crane soon learned the importance of design, with colour subservient to strong lines which would reproduce very clearly. His illustrations from the 1870s onwards, like *This Little Pig went to Market* (page 34), showed the strong outline and clear bright colours which were to become his personal trademark. Crane saw that his children's books could appeal to the poor as well as the rich. In fact the illustrators Kate Greenaway and Randolph Caldecott recognized the success of Crane's early books and adopted many of his ideas, increasing the popularity of the colour-illustrated children's book. Kate Greenaway, who was born one year later than Crane, worked with Crane's publisher Edmund Evans on her first successful children's book *Under the Window*, 1879, which was praised by Ruskin for its drawings, and sold over 100,000 copies and was translated into French and German. *Mother Goose* followed in 1881, *Little Anne* and *The Language of Flowers* in 1882. Crane met Miss Greenaway only once, although in 1876 a combination of their drawings was issued entitled *The Quiver of Love: A Collection of Valentines Ancient and Modern*.

Randolph Caldecott illustrated sixteen children's books, beginning with *The House that Jack Built* in 1878. Caldecott's style was that of a caricaturist of an eighteenth-century English countryside, with manor houses, hunting fields and peasants. Crane considered both Greenaway and Caldecott as rivals 'though in both cases their aim lies more in the direction of character study and their work is more of a pictorial character than strictly decorative' (*An Artist's Reminiscences*).

Crane's apparent success as an illustrator must have influenced the Rev. C. L. Dodgson (Lewis Carroll), who had completed *Alice in Wonderland* in 1865 and *Through the Looking Glass* in 1872, both of which were illustrated by the influential John Tenniel. Dodgson however wrote to Crane in 1878 of his displeasure with this illustrator, and offered Crane the commission for *Bruno's Revenge*, which was later to be illustrated by Henry Furniss in 1889. He offered Crane '£60 worth of work in any sizes and shapes you think proper'. More importantly, he wrote to him on his theory of design, which provides an important insight into the attitudes of Crane's contemporaries: 'You are probably more learned on the subject of ancient art than I am: but my theory is that among savages there is a much earlier stage than outline drawing – viz. mere reproduction (in clay etc.) of the solid form. I imagine that you would find idols and other representations in solid form among nations where any kind of drawing is unknown. The next step I should expect to be *alto relievo* (arising from the discovery that you can only see one side of the image at once) and this would gradually flatten down. Then the effect (with a side light) would be a flat surface with strong black outlines of shadow marking the outline of the form represented. And the next step would be to paint lines representing these shadows: and such lines would be broad at first, and would narrow on discovery that their breadth was not an essential feature. However, this is all rather theory than actual knowledge' (*An Artist's Reminiscences*).

Crane in fact had employed such a theory of line throughout his career as an illustrator, and he summarizes this theory in his book *Line and Form*, 1900. He sought a design of ordered spacings and graphic patterns to illustrate a story, with equally balanced areas of light and dark. More importantly, he used the element of line, either firm or dotted, and emphasized by colour, to unify a design and give it its expression of style. Such a style meant to Crane 'the difference between the quick and the dead'. A drawing in line was the result of a convention, a treaty between mind and nature, 'signed by the free hand of the designer, and sealed by the understanding and imagination'. Such theories of line influenced the master of penned line, Aubrey Beardsley, who wrote in 1892 of his desire to explain the importance of line, but felt Crane's article in the *Art Journal* summarized his feelings too well. Beardsley was also to publish Crane's drawings in the *Yellow Book* of 1894. To Crane, line was the skeleton in all art controlling the expression in every work (see page 6). He believed the use of line had deteriorated into a flaccid sketchiness, which did much to explain the poor state of the arts of his day. He hoped more artists would abandon the use of charcoal and chalk-smudged line in favour of the clear lines of pen and ink. He accused his contemporaries: 'If you are not forcible you can at least be black, and you can command an abundance of the convenient obscurity of shadow to hide the want of invention and the absence of purity and precision of line' (*The Claims of Decorative Art*, 1892). While teaching at the South Kensington School of Art, Crane urged his students to acknowledge the importance of clear, firm line, for a 'simple sense of fitness is all that is required as regards the appreciation of form which is the outcome of "good taste"' (*South Kensington and its Art Training*, 1912). Crane believed all book decoration, including the type or script and the cover design, should be subservient to the concept of the book as a whole. The plan, the scale of illustrations, the balance between page and drawings, and the proportions between type size and drawings, should all be taken into account for the overall design. The book illustration should not be considered merely as a simple design, capable of placement anywhere: it should be more than an accidental sketch. The ornamentation within the book could be provided by breaking a mass of type with manuscript lettering, decorative initials or accessories (page 5). Such type, in a rectangular format, has the force of a black and white design, and could be used for heavy black areas with thick type, or to lighten pages to increase readability. Crane always followed the golden rule that any area not occupied by type was a field for an accompanying or terminating design.

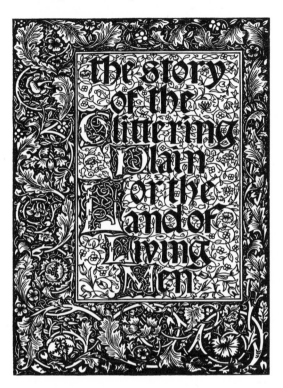

Title-page to
The Story of the Glittering Plain, 1894

The individual elements of a book's structure had to be unified in design; even the endpapers should complement the book's interior, possibly by repeating a design motif present in the illustrations (*Flora's Feast*, Plates IX–XII). The frontispiece could be more pictorial, with a rich border surrounding the type (*The Story of the Glittering Plain*, page 9). The pages of text should be treated as panels of figure design, enclosed with fanciful borders to suggest a medieval tapestry (*Faerie Queen*, pages 88–89).

The illustrators of Crane's day studied such examples of Renaissance book design as *Hypnerotomachia Poliphili*, 1499, and *Aesop's Fables*, 1493; and wood-engraved works of Charles Ricketts and Charles Shannon (*Daphnis and Chloe*, 1897, or illustrations to Oscar Wilde's *Sphinx*, 1894) show the influence of the simply-designed Renaissance interiors of these early sources. Crane concluded that '...it might be possible to construct an actual theory of the geometric relation of figure design, ornamental forms, and forms of lettering, text and type upon them, but we are more concerned with free artistic invention for the absence of which no geometric rules can compensate. The invention of the design comes first in order, the rules and principles are discovered afterwards to confirm and establish their truth – would that they did not also sometimes crystallize their vitality!' (*Of the Decorative Illustration of Books Old and New*, 1896).

The success of Crane's designs may owe much to his thorough knowledge of the engraving process, which he learned while apprenticed for three years to W. J. Linton. He wrote: 'I consider it was an advantage to me thus to have been assisted with a definite handicraft, as well as an art like wood-engraving, instead of going through the usual academic or school course' (*The Portfolio*, 1890). Crane learned not only the technical skill of the engraver at the Linton Company, but also the sad plight of the contemporary engraver. The engraver, if not phased out entirely by some process of automatic reproduction, had virtually become a slave to a process and to an artist. The artist could sketch freely in broad spontaneous strokes, heedless of their eventual placement on a page, and Crane considered his work as 'being no more than more or less adroit splashes of ink upon it, which the text, torn into an irregularly ragged edge, seems instinctively to shrink from touching, squeezing itself together like the passengers in a crowded omnibus might do, reluctantly to admit a chimney sweep' (*Of the Decorative Illustration of Books Old and New*, 1896).

The engraver's job was to transfer these sketches on to a block for reproduction by a precise linear copying of the artist's original. The typical engraver's office, in which Crane and his colleagues worked, was composed of a row of engravers and apprentices seated before a bench, with eyeglass stands and rows of gravers before them. At night a gas lamp provided the necessary light, magnified through a large water-filled glass globe. Each engraver rested his block upon a leather sand-filled bag for steadiness. An apprenticeship lasted from four to five years. After learning the various techniques one soon specialized within one particular area, either transferring designs to the block, or whitening the block with zinc white powder and water, or engraving the actual block, which was passed on to the 'first man' or 'facsimile man' who worked to complete the plate. Such division of labour allowed greater speed and perfection in the final engraving. Linton's firm was noted for engraving such important works as Christina Rossetti's poem *Goblin Market*, and engravings after Sir Frederick Leighton's paintings.

Crane, however, objected to the element of factory production in the engraver's craft, believing that the engraver's art thus became weak and purposeless. His own talent for design would have been wasted as an engraver, as Linton and his publisher Edmund Evans recognized.

Evans explained that Crane did '...all sorts of things for me...he was a genius. The only subjects which I found he could not draw were figure subjects of everyday life, such as appeared in *London Society*, a popular magazine of these days'. Evans also described the process used to reproduce Crane's illustrations for his *Toybooks*: 'They were originally drawn by Crane, the black only; the treatment of each subject was quite original, masses of black being freely used so that when the proofs were painted as a guide for the colour printer, the intention was clearly seen from the beginning: a flesh tint, a red with a fraction of brown in it, a dark blue with brown added, a yellow with raw sienna, were the only printings required to obtain a very good artistic effect. Of course the most was made of this limited scale of colouring by engraving and crossing the colours, either solid or in gradations of engraving' (*Reminiscences of Edmund Evans*).

The sense of open white space in Crane's designs links him stylistically with the new tradition of engraving practised by such illustrators as Laurence Houseman, Arthur Boyd Houghton (as in the *Graphic America* series of 1870), Charles Ricketts, and Shannon and Aubrey Beardsley. Before this time, the Pre-Raphaelite engravers believed that every square inch of their wood-engraved designs should be worked with a jewel-like effect. They regarded the wood on which they drew like a precious metal, the surface area of which should be used to the full. In the works of Houseman, Houghton and Crane (*Queen Summer*, page 83), the use of the white or black areas (which may have been coloured later) as a means of expression was exploited with maximum effect. The value of white upon black, and black upon broad areas of white, was then recognized by the emerging illustrators of the day. Crane had admired the Pre-Raphaelite designers, but more for their decorative medieval quality, as seen in the work of Rossetti in the Pre-Raphaelite periodical *The Germ*, that for their mastery of the technique of engraving.

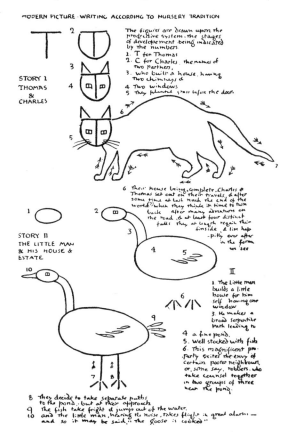

Study for drawing in the nursery tradition from *Line and Form*, 1900

Photographic engraving began to replace the more tedious technique of wood engraving, as this made possible faithful reproductions of the artist's original work. It was used for Crane's work *The First of May, A Fairy Masque*, 1881, reproducing accurately Crane's own handwriting, and delicate linear figures and borders. Crane saw the disadvantage of such a process occurring if the artist relied too much upon the reproduction.

'It has led in illustrated work to the method of painting in black and white, which has taken the place very much of the use of line...and through this has confused and deteriorated the faculty of inventive design, and the sense of ornament and line, having concentrated artistic interest on the literal realization of certain aspects of superficial facts, instantaneous impressions instead of ideas, and abstract treatment of form and line' (*Of the Decorative Illustration of Books Old and New*, 1896).

(a) Tailpiece from *Grimm's Household Stories*, 1882

(b) Design for *Sonnets of Love*

The children's books of Walter Crane are dominated by his firm belief that the imagination of a child should be continually fresh and stimulated, and his bright colourings, sensitive line and allegorical symbolism provided both child and adult of the late nineteenth century with a new sense of visual enrichment. Hitherto, children's book illustrations had not enjoyed the same importance as painting within established fine art circles. Many illustrators worked under pseudonyms in order that their paintings could be exhibited at the Royal Academy. But Crane regarded illustrating as an attractive exercise for designers with a vivid imagination who sought an acceptable outlet for their unrestricted fantasies, and wished to revolt against standards of recognized taste.

There is, therefore, an obvious difficulty in attempting a stylistic analysis of Crane's works of fantasy. However, the expressive use of line was certainly borrowed from his study of Greek pottery, and he in fact suggested to his students in *Line and Form*, 1900, that the study of Greek vases was necessary for the understanding of the purity of line. The influence of Greek vases is evident in such works as *Baby's Own Aesop* (page 71). Crane studied the Japanese print for its flat decorative quality and clarity of design, and he turned constantly to the furniture and interior decoration of the Renaissance, Dutch and eighteenth-century French periods for various elements which he incorporated in his designs for children. He recognized the austerity of medieval and Renaissance interiors, and the flamboyance of French interior and costumes, that same flamboyance which Aubrey Beardsley imitated in his drawings (*Mademoiselle de Maupin*, 1898). He disliked the sketchy impressionistic line employed by Caldecott, preferring the completely outlined contour drawing, framed with figures, and placed within a fully defined setting, often of his own invention.

It would be possible to analyse Crane's book illustrations chronologically by dividing them into three categories, viz. (1) early works, 1867–76; (2) mature work, 1877–86, and (3) works predominantly for the adult, 1887–1915. However, the brief notes given here will deal with the plates individually, with references to additional works and artists where necessary for an understanding of the artist's overall style.

Tailpiece for *Grimm's Household Stories*, 1882

I. *Little Red Riding Hood, 1874*
The range of colour was extended in these children's books with tints of yellow and red. Here pure red is used to give a vital quality to the design, while the landscape is coloured by overlapping red, blue and yellow. The book was reissued in 1898 by John Lane, along with *Jack and the Beanstalk* and *The Forty Thieves*.

II. *Beauty and the Beast, 1874*

III. *The Yellow Dwarf, 1874*
This design is important as an example of Crane's use of colour to express mood. Here the brilliant red of the witch highlights the fear expressed by the pale tones of the maiden's dresses. The bright yellow-tiled floor and tapestries decorated with faint motifs heighten the contrast between the moods. Crane's facility in describing a historical style in a simple manner is apparent in the Renaissance interior.

IV. *The Forty Thieves, 1874*

V. *King Luckieboy's Party, 1871*
The subjects of this design represent four historical periods which interested Crane and are found in his children's illustrations. The Grecian draped woman holds a pose similar to that of the Tanagra figurines popular at this time, and which Whistler and Albert Moore used in their paintings. The contemporary sailor's uniform recalled Crane's interest in this interpretation. Jack Frost's robe and hat in the Renaissance style echoes the flavour of many interior scenes and costumes in Crane's books, and the Cavalier costume is reminiscent of the Dutch influence in many Crane drawings. These drawings however differ from previous *Toybooks* in the elements of mythology and Latin phrases introduced here.

VI. *The Fairy Ship, 1871*
The radical difference in the style of this drawing betrays the influence of the Japanese print in its areas of broad black shape, and decorative patterns, and a slant-axis spatial perspective is strongly reminiscent of the compositions of contemporary impressionist paintings. The colour scheme of the illustrations at this time shows the addition of yellow and colours formed from the superimposition of yellow over red and blue.

VII. *The Baby's Bouquet, 1878*
The success of *The Baby's Opera* prompted Crane to write a sequel with nursery songs from France, Germany and England, translated by Lucy Crane. The book was followed by 1886 by *Baby's Own Aesop*, and the three books were reissued as *The Triplets* in 1899.

VIII. *Baby's Own Aesop, 1886*
Crane developed the imaginatively-shaped type block to unify his designs. Here the lily leaf establishes a formal panel composition. The crane became a symbol for Crane's work, featuring in book illustrations, friezes, tapestries, and in his signature.

Crane returned to the refined use of colour for these designs which represent Flora calling out the flowers season by season from their winter sleep. Each flower is personified and attired appropriately and poetically, from the yawning spring flowers to the opponents of King Frost with their narrow leaf lances. The drawings, which enjoyed universal appeal, were lithographed with great accuracy, delicate watercolour hues being laid in afterwards on the outline proofs. The boldness of the orange poppies is tempered by the delicate coloration of adjoining pages. The text is handwritten in Gothic characters, with motifs and colours from the drawings repeated in the illuminated initials.

A party is given for all the days of the year, each guest personified and portrayed, as here, as a curious mixture of period costumes and imaginative character associations. The style is a mixture of figures posed against expanses of blank space, rectangular blocks of text, and occasional vignettes of room interiors.

The flower figures are designed in the same style as those in *Flora's Feast*, but here often stand against a background of intricate detailed pattern, with recurring rose or lily motif. The flat colour of previous works is abandoned in favour of thin, short brush strokes executed on the lithographic plate. The lettering style of *Flora's Feast*, with text above the drawings on a white unframed background, gives way to a lettered scroll on a pure white background, gaining prominence and underlining the medieval character of the book.

26. *Sing a Song of Sixpence*, 1866
This drawing began a whole series in which Crane departed from the square bordered illustration and adopted the style of early illuminated manuscripts, introducing the text with large Gothic initial letters interwoven within the design, and using long pointed downstrokes for the body text. The book was reissued in *Song of Sixpence Toybook* in 1876.

27. *The Old Courtier*, 1867
Crane framed this picture with a Gothic archway reminiscent of the interest in the Gothic style about which John Ruskin and A. W. Pugin wrote at this time. The design in fact resembles the frontispiece engraving by T. Barry for Pugin's *Examples of Gothic Architecture*, second edition, 1850. The colour in these early books was limited to red and blue with black shading from the key block, but even then the designs were restrained and calm compared with many other books of the period.

28. *Multiplication Table in Verse*, 1867
The use of pictures in teaching children to read seemed of prime importance to Crane, who later illustrated the textbook *The Golden Primer*, 1884 for J. M. D. Meiklejohn, and *The Walter Crane Reader*, 1899, by Miss Nellie Dale. The style resembles that of newspaper or magazine artist-reporters such as those published in the *Illustrated London News*. Crane had in fact worked as a court reporter-artist during his time with W. J. Linton.

29. *Little Annie and Jack in London*, 1869
Stories of the Great Exhibition of 1851 in the Crystal Palace influenced the early Crane who studied accounts of the exhibits from articles in the *Illustrated London News* and remembered stories told him by his parents of their visit there. The drawing here shows the interior of the Crystal Palace Exhibition Hall which housed machine-made articles after the Victorian taste.

30. *Little Annie and Jack in London*, 1869
Crane was interested in the fashions of his day. As a child he would draw the costumes of the portrait models in his father's studio, and later, while working for Linton's engraving firm, he illustrated dress catalogues. Here Crane's use of firm outline, strong areas of black, and decorative pattern, indicate his interest in design, possibly gleaned from Japanese prints. The telegraph wire and view of St Paul's in the background indicate Crane's awareness of the industrialization in Victorian London. The figure of Annie is reminiscent of John Tenniel's illustrations of Alice for Lewis Caroll's *Alice in Wonderland*, 1865.

31. *King Luckieboy's Party*, 1871
The subject of this book is a humorous allegorical procession of twelve months, each month with its characteristic accessories. The book, with its compact masses of patterned detail and flat coloured background and floor, represents a change in Crane's style. The influence of his study of Japanese prints given to him by a naval friend is in evidence. The Japanese print became an important basis for the decorative designs of Crane's contemporaries Goodwin, Whistler, and later Beardsley. This drawing shows decorative bird and floral panels in the background, similar to the tapestries Crane designed with the William Morris Company, which also produced wallpapers with these designs.

32. *The Fairy Ship*, 1871

33. Endpaper to *The Fairy Ship*, 1871

34. *This Little Pig Went to Market*, 1871
The simplicity of line and flatness of form give this design a unique quality which Crane used in later works. The frontal position of the piglets and distorted floor space again recall the Japanese method of pictorial space and design.

35. *The Absurd ABC*, 1874
This design carries the concept of flattened space to its logical conclusion, with figures as silhouettes and no organized spatial scheme. Crane often utilized the inserted block for text placed in various areas of the original design. The design anticipated Crane's nursery wallpaper designs for Messrs Jeffrey and Company (1875).

36–37. *The Forty Thieves*, 1874
This book was one of the *New Toybook* series Crane designed for George Routledge priced at sixpence per paper edition, or one shilling if mounted on linen. The design makes use of architectural details which Crane developed into an archaeological exactness.

38. *The Forty Thieves*, 1874
Here the arched hallway with wood-filigreed window recalls Sir Frederick Leighton's Arab Hall at 1 Holland Park; about this time Crane designed the gold mosaic frieze in the Moorish-styled hall. Randolph Caldecott also designed the bird capitals for the columns of the room.

39. *My Mother*, 1874
This topical design incorporates a French Empire interior with figures in contemporary dress. The delicate use of *fleur de lys* wallpaper and receding flower-patterned floor shows Crane's masterful use of decoration in the portrayal of interiors. The momentary event represented may relate to the fragmented aspect of composition, typical of impressionist designs of the period.

40. Cover to *Cinderella*, 1874
The use of enamelled yellow paper for popular book covers was introduced by Edmund Evans and here used for the Routledge *New Toybook* series. The cover design by Crane remained standard for the whole series of over one hundred books. Cover designs during this period were important to the publishers for increasing book sales, since covers were often used as advertisements in shops and on posters.

41. *Cinderella*, 1874

42–43. *Cinderella*, 1874
This design incorporates a mixture of Crane's historical interests. An eighteenth-century prince in wig and waistcoat meets a Cinderella in contemporary costume watched by an audience of various nationalities, including an Oriental, a Greek Orthodox priest, a Roman legionary, a Nubian and English ladies. The sunflower gown of the woman in the foreground recalls the popular interest in the flower as a symbol of the aestheticism soon to be introduced by Oscar Wilde. The figures all stand upon a Dutch tiled floor.

44. *Puss in Boots*, 1874
This book was reissued with *Cinderella* and *Valentine and Orson*, with new additions by Crane in *Cinderella's Picture Book* in 1897.

45. *Valentine and Orson*, 1874
This story centres on the ancestry of a Renaissance king and his wife, Bellisant, sister to Pepin, King of France. Crane designed historically accurate Renaissance interiors to teach his readers, and placed figures in Pre-Raphaelite poses in forest settings.

46. *Valentine and Orson*, 1874
Here Orson is drawn with lions and a landscape background, revealing the influence of Crane's studies of early German woodcuts.

47. *The Three Bears*, 1876
Crane wrote that he liked to incorporate ideas from contemporary interior designs in his illustrations. Here the Dutch interior with its open leaded window and carved sideboard might have been taken from a Vermeer painting. The furniture and mirror are also examples of Crane's studies of historical decoration. The fleeing girl seems awkward, but Crane found that intensified figure poses seemed more appropriate for children's books than the classical figure poses of his artist colleagues, like Albert Moore.

48. Frontispiece to *Old Mother Hubbard*, 1873
Originally a Routledge *Toybook*, this book was later reissued in *Mother Hubbard, Her Picture Book*, 1897, containing *Mother Hubbard*, *The Three Bears* and *The Absurd ABC*.

49. *Old Mother Hubbard*, 1873
This book was designed while Crane was in Rome in 1871. The poodle which he used for Mrs Hubbard's dog was extremely popular in Rome at the time. The division of pictorial sequences in this design is typical of Crane's concern to unify the text with the illustration.

50. *Jack and the Beanstalk*, 1874
Originally published as *Walter Crane's Toybook, New Series*, for George Routledge. The book was reissued by John Lane, in 1898, with *Little Red Riding Hood* and *The Forty Thieves*.

51. *Jack and the Beanstalk*, 1874
The overall foliage design of this drawing is reminiscent of William Morris wallpaper, which Crane admired.

52–53. *Beauty and the Beast*, 1874
This was one of the new shilling series of *Toybooks* which Crane designed for Routledge. It was reissued by John Lane in 1901 as *Beauty and the Beast Picture Book*, with the *Frog Prince* and *The Hind in the Wood*. This design is a classic montage of Crane's decorative interests, spread across two pages of the original book.

54. *Beauty and the Beast*, 1874
The interior decoration with tapestry background recalls Crane's interest in medieval decoration. The use of eighteenth-century costumes for Beauty and her attendants is also seen in the work of Beardsley in the illustrations to his novel *Under the Hill* and the designs for *Mademoiselle de Maupin*, 1898, which include the use of a monkey attending a woman.

55. *Beauty and the Beast*, 1874
Here Crane used the lamenting, sorrowful woman of the Pre-Raphaelite painters among areas of William Morris foliage.

56. *Princess Belle Etoile*, 1875

57. *The Yellow Dwarf*, 1874
Against a tree reminiscent of those designed by William Morris, the dwarf confronts a young maiden in the popular Greek Tanagra figure pose. The background landscape with its meandering river again recalls Crane's interest in German woodcuts. The design for the dwarf derives from the plant forms which Crane was later to describe in *Flora's Feast*, 1889.

58-59. *Goody Two Shoes*, 1874
Crane blends Renaissance costumes and the thatch-roofed cottages of an English village setting into a strongly naturalistic eighteenth-century story about the lives of two orphaned girls.

60. *Bluebeard*, 1875
This book was so historically accurate in its rendering of Renaissance interiors that Crane's critics believed every child should use the book to understand the Renaissance period. The Black Knight recalls a design of Burne-Jones for his painting *Perseus and the Dragon*.

61. *Mrs. Mundi at Home*, 1875
This work marks the beginning of a new style for Crane's book illustration. Crane called the book a 'mock comical, fantastic, and allegorical medley, which incorporated contemporary attitudes of art, science and literature'. The book includes caricature portraits of Tennyson, William Morris, Swinburne, Dante Gabriel Rossetti and Robert Browning. The drawings are done in bold, firm outlines, without shading to suggest form, much as the Greek painter of vases would describe his figures. Each page has a narrow border design which echoes a motif in the drawing itself and the enclosed poem. A mild humour pervades the book, with political allusions in the final pages. It was published by Marcus Ward and Company, the firm in which Crane's brother was to become art director.

62. *Aladdin*, 1876
The design shows Crane's mastery in the use of groups of figures to create a decorative rhythm as well as to describe a pictorial sequence.

63. *The Baby's Opera*, 1877
The coloured illustrations mark the beginning of a subtler colour with wider range, including light blues, yellows, and delicate brick reds. The drawings had an unmistakable influence on Kate Greenaway whose book *Under the Window* was to establish her success as an illustrator.

64. Title page to *The Baby's Opera*, 1877
This book was the result of Crane's rejoining Evans after being rejected for further work by Routledge. The book included a combination of favourite nursery rhymes with accompanying pictures and music, which proved attractive to mothers and children. Crane's sister Lucy did the translating for the music. The five-shilling book sold 10,000 copies and was reprinted in a second edition.

LIST OF BLACK AND
WHITE ILLUSTRATIONS

65. Title page to *Grimm's Household Stories*, 1882
Inspired by his illustrations to *The Necklace of Princess Fiorimunde and other stories* by Mary A. de Morgan in 1880, Crane designed this book of stories translated by his sister Lucy. His designs are full-page drawings with decorative borders and inverted triangle-shaped tail-pieces, and show a shift in Crane's style from the decorative purity of line in earlier designs toward a more pictorial style.

66. '*The Sleeping Beauty*' from *Grimm's Household Stories*, 1882
This design shows figures in Pre-Raphaelite poses. The decorative framework of medallions is similar to the gilt frames designed by Rossetti and his colleagues.

67. *Pan Pipes*, 1883
This book is a collection of old songs which Crane illustrated in colour. Crane wanted to use his own invented musical type-style since he felt the unity of the pages was broken by the conventional ones. The book was designed in an oblong shape, for easy handling at the piano, and the songs were arranged by Theodore Marzials. The song *The Three Ravens* was designed using the lamenting figure poses of Pre-Raphaelite painters like Holman Hunt.

68. *Pothooks and Perseverance*, 1885
In this book Crane's inventive wordplay and drawings are an attempt to encourage children to persevere in the study of learning fundamentals. The story tells of the struggle of the boy knight Percy Vere (*persevere*), with the ABC Dragon. The illustrations are done in the style of vignettes, with sparse areas shaded in watercolour, and only slight definition to the background.

69. *Little Queen Anne and Her Majesty's letters*, 1885
This book, in the style of *Pothooks and Perseverance*, also shares its intention of teaching children through the association of words and delightful pictures.

   Queen Anne is preparing for a costume ball. Dressed as Athena, she meets such familiar friends as The Three R's, who are imaginatively drawn with their appropriate accessories. The 'Riting' character skates upon pen quills, carrying an ink horn and quill, and wearing a duck-feather hat. Crane uses historical costuming combined with imaginative fantasy to engage the reader's interest.

70–71. *Baby's Own Aesop*, 1886
Crane, who believed good book design to include all aspects of the book, knew the importance of the cover design. Perhaps the French-printed colour poster luring prospective buyers was the inspiration for such a conscious effort by illustrators to design an appealing book cover. This book with its short text and large illustrations was designed to appeal to the railway traveller. The design is based upon classical motifs: the Doric-columned porch, the youth in Greek garb, and the overall formal balance.

72. *The Sirens Three*, 1886
Each design for Crane's poem was developed from suggestions within the text. The fluid stream of figures here suggested the flow of life, described by Crane as 'the vivid and significant imagery, the oriental richness and colour, the pathetic or satiric philosophy, and its extraordinary modern touches and general aptness of its reflections on life' (*An Artist's Reminiscences*). The *Rubá'iyát of Omar Khayyám*, in an original edition owned by William Morris, was the prototype for Crane's poems.

21

73. *The Sirens Three*, 1886
Crane's poem was written and illustrated for publication in instalments in *The English Illustrated Magazine*, and was later issued as a complete book by Macmillan. Crane used a medieval-style lettering with a Greek vine motif in the right corner, as seen here. The subject for this design, *Freedom*, was taken from the composition of a painting by Crane exhibited at the Grosvenor Gallery, now in the William Morris Gallery, Walthamstow. Here the winged Freedom appears before the allegorical figures of Bondage and Old Age.

74. *The Sirens Three*, 1886
This design exploits Crane's mastery of the classical draped figure for decorative design. The decorative border used Greek egg-and-dart moulding, combined with putty, stretched to fill the interstices of a volute border. Crane believed figures should be used to fill a prescribed space, a theory also demonstrated in his decorative frieze work of this period. The handwritten script was inspired by the line of the Greek vase painter.

75. *Legends for Lionel*, 1887
This book is one of a group Crane designed for his son. His designs were derived from fantasies which he developed by drawing various objects in universal combinations (see page 15). The drawings are reminiscent of John Tenniel's work in Lewis Carroll's *Through the Looking Glass*, 1872.

76. *Birthday Invitation*, 1897
Crane remained dedicated to his family throughout his career, using his talent for illustrating to amuse them, or to announce to his friends an important family event. He often followed the advice of his children in gauging the potential of his book designs.

77. Cover to *Echoes of Hellas*, 1887
These illustrations were first suggested to Crane by a series of dramatic productions arranged by such artists as Lord Leighton, C. F. Watts and Henry Holiday. The author of the productions and script, George Warr, invited Crane to revise the productions and redesign the costume and scenery for a performance given by the actresss Dorothy Dene.

78. *Echoes of Hellas: The Odyssey*, 1887
The book was divided into three parts: *The Tale of Troy*, *The Wandering of Ulysses* and *The Story of Orestes*. The total design of the book was done by Crane. He kept the character of his original designs by drawing each plate directly on a lithographic zinc plate, which was printed in black and terracotta tones. This colour scheme was suggested to him by ancient Greek vases.

79. *The Happy Prince*, 1888
Crane was the friend of Oscar Wilde at the time when Wilde was editor of the periodical *Woman's World* in which he praised Crane's work. He persuaded Crane to illustrate this collection of his children's stories. *The Happy Prince* is the tale of a golden statue which eventually strips itself of gold and gives it to the poor and in this way manages to find happiness.

80. *The Happy Prince: The Selfish Giant*, 1888
The Selfish Giant is the story of a giant who finds happiness by allowing little children to play in his garden. Here the child personifies the giant's discovery of Christ. The book

includes three full-page illustrations by Crane, and decorative pieces by George Jacob Hood. The latter afterwards illustrated the second edition in 1902.

81. Title page to *The Children of the Castle*, 1890
     Crane designed a series of Mrs Molesworth's novels. This title page combines the linear style of the border figure prevalent in his later works with the small vignette castle scene in his earlier tight-lined style.

82. Frontispiece to *The Children of the Castle*, 1890
     In this illustration the fluid lines of Crane's style are used to portray movement and a forbidding mood of fear. The book was one of over a hundred books written by Mrs Molesworth for both children and adults.

83. *Queen Summer, or the Tournament of the Rose*, 1891
     The medieval theme of this book is manifest in all the illustrations. Queen Summer is holding court in a flower garden, when a dispute arises between the Rose and the Lily over which is superior in beauty. The powerful linear silhouette of the Queen against a blank background is reminiscent of the distinct fluidity of Art Nouveau decoration popular at this time.

84–85. *Queen Summer*, 1891
        The dispute between the Lily and the Rose becomes a tournament joust, with the champions of both sides and their horses decked in appropriately decorated armour and trappings. The flat design and subdued colour was suggested by medieval tapestry designs which Crane and Morris had already adapted for their wallpaper and hanging designs.

86. *The Story of the Glittering Plain*, 1894
     This book was the result of Crane's collaboration with William Morris, the founder of the Kelmscott Press. Crane designed the 23 small square illustrations which Morris surrounded with a decorative border in the style of his tapestry designs. Crane adapted the style of sixteenth-century Italian and German woodcuts with bold-lined figures portrayed against a receding landscape. The book was printed by Morris's Kelmscott Press, which had produced an earlier version in 1891 as its first published book. This later edition was printed in a mixture of Troy and Chaucer styles of type-faces designed by Morris and printed in black and red.

87. Title page to *The History of Reynard the Fox*, 1894
     Elaborate borders unifying the overall book design were believed by one critic to be unique to Crane. Before him borders often bore little relation to the text or illustrations they surrounded and were designed quite independently. The frontispiece and title-page borders of this book are taken from *The History of Reynard the Fox*.

88–89. *Spenser's Faerie Queen*, 1894
        It was felt that this subject, originally suggested to Crane by George Allan, would appeal to the many followers of John Ruskin at this time. The work, in three volumes representing three years' work, was considered by some to be Crane's masterpiece. His designs, a series of diverse figured types in mythological and allegorical settings, were criticized for their dated appearance, for they lacked the elements of local colour which Dürer would have used. However, the interrelationship between illustration and border reveals Crane's mastery of a unified design.

The illustrations themselves are based upon the original text edited by T. J. Wise, but Crane made use of the decorative borders for his own imaginative interpretation of the themes. The book was arranged in six parts, divided into twelve *canti* in each of the three volumes, which were issued at intervals between 1894 and 1896.

90. *Shakespeare's Two Gentlemen of Verona*, 1894
This style belongs to Crane's later illustrations. There is less concern for the clarity aimed for in his earlier interiors: the line here is flatter, yet richly shaded to suggest depth. The narrative character of his illustrations seems to gain importance in these works; the sketchy linear tapestry background is in marked contrast to the sharply defined tapestry background of *Beauty and the Beast* (page 50).

91. *Shakespeare's The Merry Wives of Windsor*, 1895
Here Crane exploited the values of tone to balance the darkened background and intricately drawn figure in the foreground. In addition to these illustrations to Shakespeare, he later completed light drawings for *The Tempest* in 1902 and drawings for *Flowers from Shakespeare's Garden, A Posy from the Plays* in 1906.

92. Cover to *A Floral Fantasy in an Old English Garden*, 1899
The silhouettes of this cover design are reminiscent of the Art Nouveau style then popular. The book was intended for a more mature reader and, along with *Flora's Feast, The Flower Wedding, Queen Summer, Flowers in a Shakespeare Garden* and *A Masque of Days*, proved very popular in the United States. In 1891–2 Crane's work was exhibited in Boston, Philadelphia, Chicago and St Louis.

93. *Spenser's The Shepheard's Calendar*, 1889
The twelve designs in this calendar are considered to be among Crane's best illustrations. Their linear style recalls the woodcut technique, with half-tones defined by small areas of dotted line. The title page is spread over two pages, a technique Crane believed important to the overall unity of the design of the book. The text is surrounded by an intricate border of mythological and historical figures which recur in the illustrations of the months.

94. *Don Quixote*, 1907
Crane continued to illustrate children's stories throughout his life. His illustrations for Judge Parry's adaptation of the Cervantes classic comprise eleven full-colour plates, originally executed in watercolour. He followed these designs with colour plates for Henry Gilbert's books *King Arthur's Knights* in 1911, *Robin Hood and the Men of Greenwood*, 1912, *The Knights of the Round Table* and *Robin Hood and his Merry Men* in 1915, the final year of Crane's life. The original drawings for *Don Quixote* are now in the Victoria and Albert Museum.

95–96. *Cartoons for the Cause*, 1886–96
Crane's socialist leanings are here represented in a series of drawings which he contributed at regular intervals to the socialist periodicals *Justice* and *The Commonweal*. Because of both their visual aspect and their success as political propaganda these designs were published in a souvenir edition of the *International Socialist Workers and Trade Union Congress* of 1896. Their style resembles that of Sir John Tenniel's later work. Although Crane worked for the socialist cause, he believed the need for socialism and understanding of the issues involved were misunderstood in his day.

Cock Robin, 1866

Sing a Song of Sixpence, 1866

AN old song made by an aged old pate,
Of an old worshipful Gentleman who
    had a great estate,
That kept a brave old house at a
    bountiful rate,
And an old Porter to relieve the poor at
    his gate;
Like an Old Courtier of the Queen's,
And the Queen's Old Courtier.

The Old Courtier, 1867

Twice FIVE are TEN Steam Boats,
Anchored in Plymouth Sound.

Multiplication Table in Verse, 1867

It was difficult, really, to get them
    away,
In time to get rested for seeing next
    day
The Sydenham Palace (that hot-house
    of ours,
Where presents and pantomimes spring
    up like flowers);
And there they heard songs, and saw
    acrobats tumble
(So certain to break all their bones if
    they stumble);
And all seemed so sparkling, bright-
    coloured, and light,
That they said, "Here's a place where
    it never is night."

Little Annie and Jack in London, 1869

And Papa and Mamma took them home the same day,—
They were glad to go home, and yet wanted to stay;
But the train went quite fast, and it seemed a nice change
To be back in their own home, where nothing was strange;

And always they reckon'd that seeing these sights
Was a thing to remember—a week of delights;
And, though they may see them all many times more,
They'll never enjoy them so much, I am sure.

Little Annie and Jack in London, 1869

Arch April came after, with
bow and with smile;
And—"If they'd allow her,
Miss Sunshiny Shower,"
Arrayed like a sunbeam, in
elegant style.

King Luckieboy's Party, 1871

Raisins in the Cabin;

The Fairy Ship, 1871

THE FAIRY SHIP

Endpaper to *The Fairy Ship*, 1871

This Little Pig Went to Market, 1871

The Absurd ABC, 1874

wife, finding that her husband did not return, went to
tell Ali Baba, who at once set off to go to the cave, and
on entering it discovered his brother's remains, which he
carried home on one of his asses, loading the other two
with bags of gold. Ali Baba then buried the body, and
contrived, with the assistance of an intelligent slave
named Morgiana, to make every one believe that Cassim
had died a natural death. Ali Baba then married the
widow, and became very rich and prosperous.

    Meanwhile the forty robbers visited their cave, and find-
ing that Cassim's body had been removed, determined
not to rest until they had discovered their enemy; and

The Forty Thieves, 1874

one of them undertaking the search, in which he was assisted by the Cobbler who had sewn Cassim's body together, at last found Ali Baba's house, which he marked with a piece of chalk, and returned to his fellows. When Morgiana saw the mark, she chalked several other doors in the same manner. The thieves then coming to attack the house, and not being able to distinguish it from the others, had to return to their cave; and the robber, who they thought had misled them, was put to death. Another robber then undertook the enterprise, and, being guided by the Cobbler, marked the door with red chalk, but Morgiana marked the neighbours' doors in the same

manner, and so defeated them a second time; and the second robber was put to death. The Captain then went into the town himself, and having found and carefully observed Ali Baba's house, returned to his men, and ordered them to buy nineteen mules and thirty-eight leathern jars, one full of oil and the rest empty. This they did, and the Captain placing one of his men in each of the empty jars, loaded the asses with them, and drove them into the town to Ali Baba's house. Ali Baba received him hospitably; and the Captain ordered his men, who remained in their jars in the yard, to come out in the middle of the night at a signal from him. He

The Forty Thieves, 1874

Who sat and watched my infant head,
When sleeping on my cradle bed
And tears of sweet affection shed?

My Mother.

When pain and sickness made me cry,
Who gazed upon my heavy eye,
And wept for fear that I should die?

My Mother.

My Mother, 1874

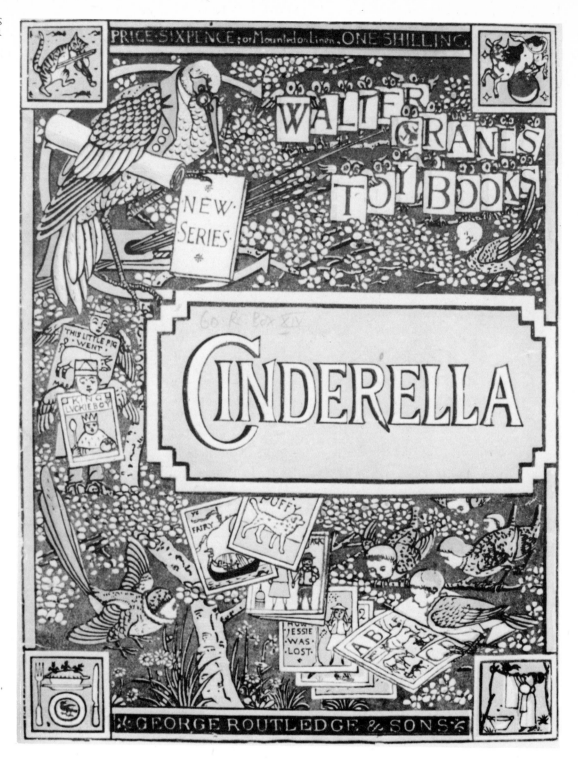

Cover to *Cinderella*, 1874

THERE was an honest gentleman, who had a daughter
    dear ;
His wife was dead, he took instead a new one in a year :
She had two daughters—Caroline and Bella were their names ;
They called the other daughter Cinderella, to their shames.
Because she had to clean the hearths and black-lead all the
    grates ;
She also had to scrub the floors, and wash the dinner plates.
But though the others went abroad, did nothing, smiled, and
    drest,
Yet Cinderella all the time was prettiest and best.
The King who ruled in that country, he had an only son,
Who gave a ball to all the town, when he was twenty-one ;
And Caroline and Bella were invited, and they said,
"Cinderella shall leave scrubbing, and act as ladies' maid."

Cinderella, 1874

And then the Fairy raised her wand, and touched the shabby
    gown—
It turned to satin, trimmed with lace, and jewels, and swans-
    down.
Her face was clean, her gloves were new, her hair was nicely
    curled,
And on her feet were shoes of glass, the neatest in the world.
" Now, Cinderella, you may go; but take care to return
Before the clock strikes twelve, or else you'll see your carriage
    turn
Into a pumpkin once again, your horses into mice;
Your coachman, footmen, will become rat, lizards, in a trice,
And you yourself the cinder-girl will once again become;
So mind that when the clock strikes twelve you must be safe
    at home."

Cinderella, 1874

42

She promised, and with joyful heart she gained the palace
    hall,
And danced, and laughed, and looked indeed the fairest of
    them all.
The King's son danced with her, and praised her lovely shape
    and air;
All treated her as if she were the greatest lady there:
But in good time she slipped away, and waited safe at home,
In kitchen corner sitting till her sisters back should come;
And when they came they told her all about the stranger fair,
And what she wore, and how she looked, and how she did
    her hair.
Next night another ball was held—the sisters dressed, and
    went,
And pretty Cinderella, too, by Godmother was sent.

"No, Master," said Puss, "give me boots to my
feet—
A pair of top-boots—and please leave me alive,
And you shall just see how we'll flourish and
thrive."

Puss in Boots, 1874

Off he ran, and Red Riding Hood went on
But often she lingered and played
And made as she went quite a pretty nosegay
With the wild flowers that grew in the glade.

I. Little Red Riding Hood

II. Beauty and the Beast

III. The Yellow Dwarf

Ali Baba's son, who one day invited him to his father's house. On hearing that the new guest would eat no salt with his meat, Morgiana's suspicions were aroused, and she recognised him as the captain of the robbers. After dinner she undertook to perform a dance before the company, and at the end of it pointed a dagger at the captain, and then plunged it into his heart. Ali Baba was very much shocked, until Morgiana explained the reasons for her conduct; he then gave her to his son in marriage, and they lived in great prosperity and happiness ever after.

IV. The Forty Thieves

November the next, arm-in-
arm with the Archer
Who shot at the froggie;
Miss Rayne Dullan Foggie,
And Mr. Jack Frost in a stick-
up and starcher.

December came last, and he
seem'd very old;
And he rode on a goat,
In a very thick coat,
Sprinkled over with snow, and
looking so cold.

V. King Luckie-Boy's Party

For me, for me, for me!
And it was deeply
laden
With good things
for me!

VI. The Fairy Ship

VII. The Baby's Bouquet

The Fox & the Crane

You have heard how Sir
        Fox treated Crane:

With soup in a plate. When again
They dined, a long bottle
Just suited Crane's throttle;
And Sir Fox licked the outside
                in vain.

·THERE·ARE·GAMES·THAT·TWO·CAN
        PLAY· AT·

VIII. Baby's Own Aesop

The little Lilies of the Vale,
White ladies delicate & pale;

IX. Flora's Feast

The Daffodil his trumpet blows
And after Spring a
hunting
goes.

X. Flora's Feast

Then lilies, turned to Tigers, blaze
Amid the garden's tangled maze.

XI. Flora's Feast

n scarlet Poppy-heads a-blaze:

XII. Flora's Feast

good Days, bad Days
were so shuffled to
gether, to the con:
founding of all sober
horoscopy.   He had
stuck the Twenty-First
of June next to the Twen-
ty-Second of December,
and the former looked
like a Maypole siding
a marrow-bone.

XIII. A Masque of Days

April Fool (as my young lord's jester) took upon himself to marshal the guests, and wild work he made with it. It would have posed old Erra Pater to have found out any given Day in the year, to erect a scheme upon —

XIV. A Masque of Days

XV. Queen Summer

And spread with 'broidered hangings gay,
Till all was ready for the fray.

XVI. Queen Summer

And as she fled, weighed down by grief and
                              sense of cruel scorn,
Lo, in the forest two fair sons to Bellisant were
                                              born ;
But while her servant went to buy some food, a
                                    great she-bear
Came up, and carried off one child unto her
                                  distant lair.
Poor Bellisant ran after her, with many a sigh
                                and moan ;
In vain,—and when she turned again, the other
                          child was gone !

Valentine and Orson, 1874

But Orson threw the Green Knight down, and
                bound him with a chain,
And set the lady free; both brothers then
                        start off to gain
The Green Knight's castle-gates,—two roaring
                    lions kept guard there,
But down they crouched when they beheld the
                        brothers void of fear.

Valentine and Orson, 1874

And, as the door stood open, in walked boldly,
  This child, whose name was Silverlocks, I'm
There was nobody there to treat her coldly, told;
  No friend to call her back, no nurse to scold.
She found herself within a parlour charming;
  And there upon the table there were placed
Three basins, sending up a smell so warming,
  That she at once felt hungry, and must taste.
The largest basin first, but hot and biting
  The soup was in it, and the second too;
The smallest basin tasted so inviting,
  That up she ate it all, with small ado.

And next she saw three chairs, and tried to sit in
  The biggest, but it was too hard and high;
The middle one she scarcely seemed to fit in,
  But in the smallest chair sat easily;
And rocked herself, her ease and comfort taking,
  Singing the pretty songs she knew so well;
When, oh! the little chair cracked loud, and, breaking,
  Gave way all suddenly, and down she fell.

They rushed upstairs, and Father Bruin, growling,
  Cried out, "Who's lain upon my bed?"
"Who's lain, on mine?" cried Mother Bruin, howling;

So Silverlocks, in sudden terror flying,
  Reached home; and when the Nurse the story hears,
She says, "You are in luck, there's no denying,
  To get away in safety from

THREE BEARS."

The Three Bears, 1876

Frontispiece to *Old Mother Hubbard*, 1873

She went to the tailor's
    To buy him a coat,
But when she came back,
    He was riding a goat.

She went to the cobbler's
    To buy him some shoes,
But when she came back,
    He was reading the news.

Old Mother Hubbard, 1873

Down the bean-stalk home he hastened, and
    upon the magic pelf
Long he lived, his mother also, till at last he
    found himself
Quite inclined for greater riches, as he knew
    an easy road;
Up he climbed the bean-stalk ladder, and
    returned with *such* a load!
But the giant nearly wakened with the bark-
    ing of a dog,—
(Very lucky 'twas for Jack, that way of sleep-
    ing like a log).

Jack and the Beanstalk, 1874

Bags of gold and silver Jack took
  home, but still his mind did lean
Towards another prize, and journey
  up the lucky stalk of bean.
Hidden in his usual corner in the
  giant's house, he spied,
Bought for that great man's amuse-
  ment, playing sweetly by his side
While he slept, a golden harp, which
  Jack at once caught up, and ran,
But the harp with human voice cried,
  "Master, master, stop this man!"
But so tipsy was the giant, though
  he tried to run and bawl,
That, with all his pains, he could not
  stop the flight of Jack at all.

Jack and the Beanstalk, 1874

Beauty and the Beast, 1874

52

Beauty and the Beast, 1874

Beauty and the Beast, 1874

Princess Belle Etoile, 1875

The Yellow Dwarf, 1874

Goody Two Shoes, 1874

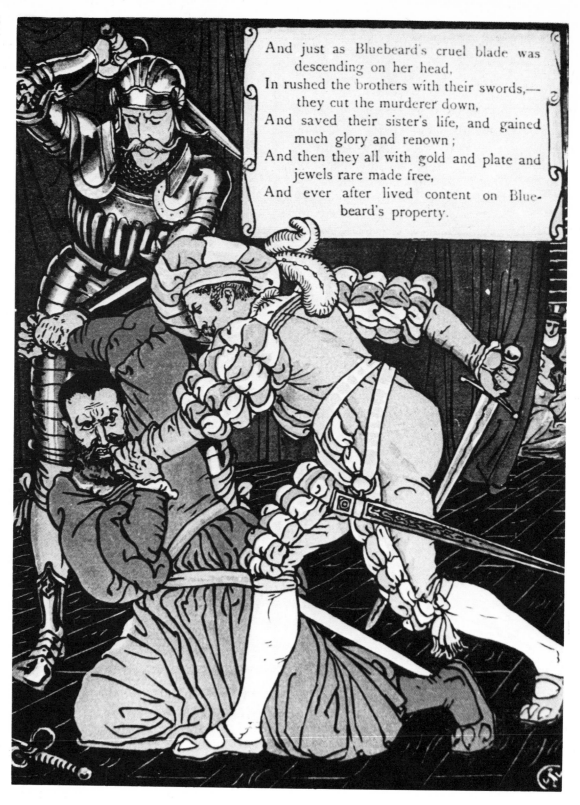

And just as Bluebeard's cruel blade was
    descending on her head,
In rushed the brothers with their swords,—
    they cut the murderer down,
And saved their sister's life, and gained
    much glory and renown;
And then they all with gold and plate and
    jewels rare made free,
And ever after lived content on Blue-
    beard's property.

Bluebeard, 1875

SOL

THE EARLIEST GUEST, AS I UNDERSTAND,
WAS THE GREAT LORD SOL, FOUR & TWENTY IN HAND.

Mrs. Mundi at Home, 1875

Aladdin, 1876

The Baby's Opera, 1877

Title-page to *The Baby's Opera*, 1877

The Baby's Opera, 1877

Title-page to Grimm's Household Stories, 1882

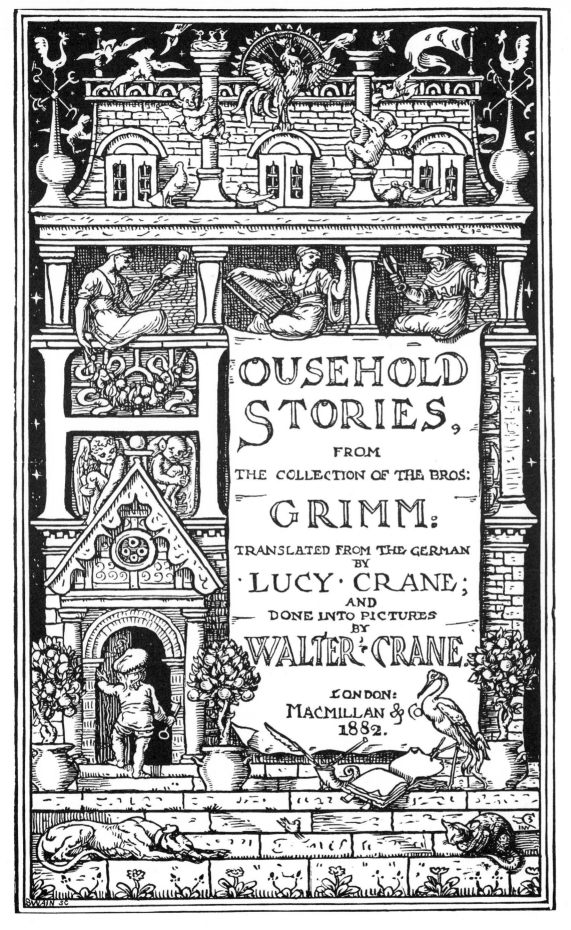

OUSEHOLD
STORIES,

FROM
THE COLLECTION OF THE BROS:

GRIMM:

TRANSLATED FROM THE GERMAN
BY
·LUCY·CRANE;
AND
DONE INTO PICTURES
BY

WALTER CRANE.

LONDON:
MACMILLAN & Cᵒ
1882.

'The Sleeping Beauty' from *Grimm's Household Stories*, 1882

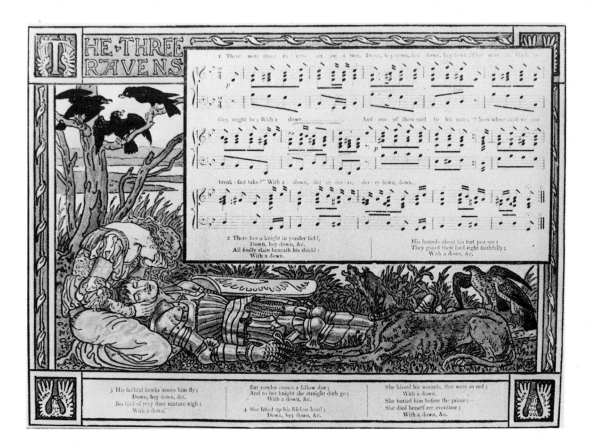

Pan Pipes, 1883

Pothooks and Perseverance, 1885

*Little Queen Anne and Her
Majesty's letters, 1885*

Baby's Own Aesop, 1886

FORTVNE·AND·THE·BOY:

A Boy heedless slept by the well
By Dame Fortune awaked, truth to tell,
Said she, "Hadst been drowned,
'T would have surely been found
This by Fortune, not Folly befel."
FORTUNE·IS·NOT·ANSWERABLE·FOR·OUR·WANT·OF·FORESIGHT

Baby's Own Aesop, 1886

CIX.

PROTEAN life which man doth vain pursue
From youth's green meads to ages' mountain's blue
The painted fly a breathless child doth chase —
Through all its changing shapes to change but true.

CX.

This quivering bubble, dyed with every stain
Of splendour & of passion, why in vain —
Ah! why? — It sails the summer air —
An iridescent moment lost in rain?

The Sirens Three, 1886

LXXIII.

SO Man, held hand & foot, a slave behold
Between the soldier-king & priest of old;
By force & fraud bound fast as by two chains—
How long, O Man, how long shall they thee hold?

The Sirens Three, 1886

LXXXI

ALL these I saw, as on time's painted page
The figure of man's life from age to age
Was figured like his life of years & hours,
And glassed his face - an infant or a mage.

LXXXII.

In boyhood bright beneath the Grecian sun,
I saw him stand, intent his race to run -
To touch the golden goal of thought & art,
And daring all man since hath dared or done.

LXXXIII.

The apple of his life to Beauty's hand
Freely he gave, & she so dowered his land,
That still tha fond world takes it for her glass,
And gazes, leaving knowledge & command.

The Sirens Three, 1886

Legends for Lionel, 1887

Birthday Invitation, 1897

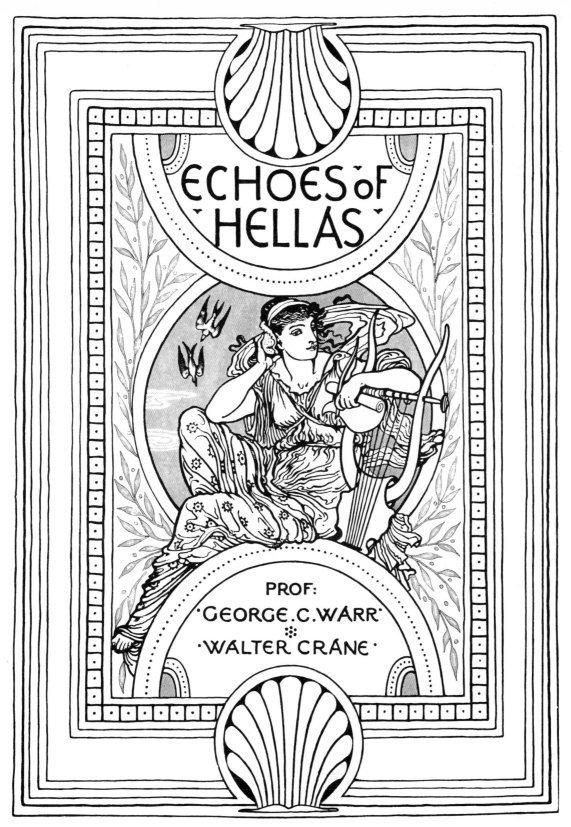

ECHOES of HELLAS

PROF:
·GEORGE·C·WARR·
※
·WALTER·CRANE·

Cover to *Echoes of Hellas*, 1887

Echoes of Hellas: The Odyssey, 1887

The Happy Prince, 1888

The Happy Prince: The Selfish Giant, 1888

THE ·CHILDREN·
·OF·THE·CASTLE·
·BY·

·MRS·MOLESWORTH·

ILLUSTRATED· BY·
·WALTER·CRANE·

LONDON: MDCCCXCIX
·MACMILLAN·&·CO·
ST. MARTIN'S ST.

Title-page to *The Children of the Castle*, 1890

"Are— are you a mermaid, or a-
that other thing ?' asked the
child. "   P. 156.

Frontispiece to *The Children of the Castle*, 1890

Whereof the grass undur was rife,
As surged & rolled the Floral strife,
With checquered fortune o'er the green,
Until at last up – rose the Queen:

Queen Summer, or the Tournament of the Rose, 1891

And as the winds about them played,
And shook the flowers or disarrayed

Queen Summer, 1891

84

Came first the glowing Rose in view,
With crimson pennon fluttering new;
With glittering spines all armed he came,
With lance and shield - a rose aflame;
With tossing crest and mantling free,
On fiery steed, - a sight to see!

Queen Summer, 1891

Chapter XIII. Hallblithe beholdeth the woman who loveth him ✿ ✿

BUT on the morrow the men arose, & the Sea-eagle and his damsel came to Hallblithe; for the other two damsels were departed, and the

The Story of the Glittering Plain, 1894

Title-page to *The History of Reynard the Fox*, 1894

Spenser's Faerie Queen, 1894

The knight with that old Dragon fights
Two days incessantly:
The third him overthrowes, and gayns
Most glorious victory.

Spenser's Faerie Queen, 1894

Shakespeare's Two Gentlemen of Verona, 1894

Shakespeare's The Merry Wives of Windsor, 1895

Cover to *A Floral Fantasy in an Old English Garden*, 1899

Spenser's The Shepheard's Calendar, 1889

Don Quixote, 1907

Cartoons for the Cause, 1886–96

Cartoons for the Cause, 1886–96

Decorative book heading, 1887

·CATALOGUE·OF·BOOKS·ILLUSTRATED·OR· ·WRITTEN·BY·CRANE·

The following list of books either written or illustrated by Crane was compiled from entries in the British Museum Readers' Catalogue, Gertrude Masse's *A Bibliography of First Editions of Books Illustrated by Walter Crane*, 1923, the catalogues of prints and drawings of the Victoria and Albert Museum and *The Art of Walter Crane*, by C. F. Konody, 1902. The British Museum catalogue was the final authority in cases of discrepancy of dates. The present list does not claim to include every book illustrated by Crane, but includes all the titles to which the author refers.

1863   *The New Forest, its History and Scenery* by John R. Wise.
       63 illustrations drawn by Walter Crane, engraved by W. J. Linton, Smith and Elder, London.

1864   *Stories from Memel for the Young* by Mrs Agnes de Havilland (née Molesworth).

       Six full-page woodcut illustrations by Walter Crane, William Hunt, London.
       Walter Crane designed between 40 and 50 *Toybooks* for various publishers between 1865 and 1886. Frederick Warne's *Toybooks*, of which Crane designed six, were rapidly copied by George Routledge. The following is a list of Warne's *Sixpenny Toybooks* and Routledge's *Sixpenny* and *Shilling Toybooks*, the latter printed by Edmund Evans and representing two-thirds of Crane's work for them. The *Sixpenny Toybooks* were small, paperbound books with eight pages of full-colour illustrations and text. The later *Shilling Toybooks* were slightly larger with eight full-page illustrations; the text was no longer incorporated but printed on separate sheets. These books always had a double-page illustration in the centre. The quality of colour showed a marked improvement in 1871 with *King Luckieboy's Party* and again in 1875 with the *Shilling Toybooks*.

1865–66 *Sixpenny Toybooks* published by Frederick Warne: *Sing a Song of Sixpence, Farmyard Alphabet, Cock Robin, The Railroad Alphabet, The House that Jack Built, Dame Trot and her Comical Cat,* and *The Waddling Frog.*

1867   *Sixpenny Toybooks* published by George Routledge: *Chattering Jack, How Jessie was Lost,* and *1, 2 Buckle My Shoe.*

1867–68 Further *Sixpenny Toybooks* by Routledge: *The Old Courtier, Multiplication Table in Verse, Grammar in Rhyme*, and *Annie and Jack in London*.

1869 *The Magic of Kindness or The Wondrous story of the Good Huan* by the Brothers Mayhew. Eight full-page illustrations by Walter Crane, Cassell, London.

1870–74 *Sixpenny Toybooks* published by George Routledge: *King Luckieboy's Party, This Little Pig Went to Market, The Fairy Ship, Old Mother Hubbard, My Mother, The Forty Thieves, The Absurd ABC, Jack and the Beanstalk, Cinderella, Valentine and Orson, Little Red Riding Hood, Puss in Boots, The Alphabet of Old Friends, Baby's Own Alphabet, The Frog Prince, The Hind in the Wood* and *The Sleeping Beauty*.

1874 *Walter Crane's New Toybook*, Routledge, London.

Walter Crane's Picturebook, Routledge, London.
Both these books contained 64 pages of designs.

1874–76 *Shilling Toybooks* published by George Routledge: *Goody Two Shoes, Beauty and the Beast, The Yellow Dwarf, Bluebeard, Princess Belle Etoile*, and *Aladdin*.

1875 *Mrs. Mundi at Home, The Terrestrial Ball*
24 illustrations by Walter Crane, Marcus Ward, London.

Tell me a Story by Mrs Molesworth, Macmillan, London.

1876 *The Quiver of Love: A Collection of Valentines Ancient and Modern*
Eight colour illustrations from drawings by Walter Crane and Kate Greenaway, Marcus Ward, London.
Crane never considered these designs reproduced satisfactorily since they were copied on a stone and lost much of their original character in the lithographic process.

1877 *The Baby's Opera, A Book of Old Rhymes with New Dresses. The Music by the Earliest Masters*
Engraved and printed in colour by Edmund Evans, Routledge, London. Bound between stiff glazed boards, and unique among the five-shilling cloth-bound books with gold designs, this book's first edition of 10,000 was reprinted a second time.

The Cuckoo Clock by Ennis Graham.
Seven plates drawn by Walter Crane, Macmillan, London.

1878 *The Baby's Bouquet, A Fresh Bunch of Old Rhymes and Tunes*
Tunes collected and arranged by Lucy Crane and colour decorations by Walter Crane. Printed by Edmund Evans, Marcus Ward, London.
This volume was issued the next Christmas as a companion work to *The Baby's Opera*.

Grandmother Dear: A Book for Boys and Girls by Mrs Molesworth.
Illustrated with seven plates by Walter Crane, Macmillan, London.

1879 *The Tapestry Room. A Child's Romance* by Mrs Molesworth.
Illustrated with seven plates by Walter Crane, Macmillan, London.

1880 *The Necklace of Princess Fiorimunde and other Stories* by Mary A. de Morgan.
Illustrations and cover by Walter Crane, Macmillan, London.

Mary A. de Morgan was the sister of William de Morgan, noted potter and ceramic designer who had hitherto designed his sister's books.

1881   *The First of May, A Fairy Masque* by J. R. Wise.
56 pencil designs by Walter Crane, printed by Goupil and Company, H. Southeran, London.
This lavish book, which took Crane three years to design, was his second collaboration with J. R. Wise (cf. *The New Forest*, 1863).

The Adventure of Heir Baby by Mrs Molesworth.
Twelve illustrations by Walter Crane, Macmillan, London.

1882   *Household Stories from the Collection of the Brothers Grimm*
Translated by Lucy Crane.
Eleven full-page plates and 108 head and tailpieces, Macmillan, London.

Rosy by Mrs Molesworth.
Seven illustrations by Walter Crane, Macmillan, London.

Routledge's Christmas Number
Stories by Mrs F. Locker, L. M. Alcott, R. M. Jephson and others, with illustrations by R. Caldecott, Kate Greenaway, Walter Crane and others, Routledge, London.

1883   *Pan Pipes. A Book of Old Songs*
Newly arranged and with accompaniments by Theodore Marzials. Colour illustrations designed by Walter Crane, engraved and printed by Edmund Evans, Routledge, London.

Us. An Old Fashioned Story by Mrs Molesworth.
Seven illustrations by Walter Crane, Macmillan, London.

1884   *Christmas Tree Land* by Mrs Molesworth.
Seven illustrations by Walter Crane, Macmillan, London.

Thoughts in a Hammock by Walter Crane.
Six full-page illustrations reproduced in *The English Illustrated Magazine*, November 1884.
The figure in a hammock at the top of page 86 is a portrait of the artist.

The Golden Primer by Prof. J. M. D. Meiklejohn, Parts I and II, 2 volumes.
32 full-page colour illustrations by Walter Crane, Blackwood, London.

1885   *Folk and Fairy Tales* by Mrs Burton Harrison.
24 illustrations by Walter Crane, Ward and Downey, London.

Slateandpencilvania: Being the Adventures of Dick on a Desert Island
'Decyphered' by Walter Crane, Marcus Ward, London.

Little Queen Anne and Her Majesty's letters
'Penned and Pictured' by Walter Crane, Marcus Ward, London.

Pothooks and Perseverance, or the ABC Serpent
'Penned and Pictured' by Walter Crane, Marcus Ward, London.
These last three books were also reissued in 1886 as a reprint under one cover called *A Romance of the Three R's.*

1886 *Baby's Own Aesop, Being the Fables Condensed in Rhyme*
Morals pictorially painted by Walter Crane, engraved and printed by Edmund Evans,
Routledge, London.
Baby's Own Aesop, *The Baby's Opera* and *The Baby's Bouquet* were reprinted under one title,
Triplets, in 1894 by Routledge.

The Sirens Three, a poem by Walter Crane.
41 pages of illustrations and decorative borders by Walter Crane, Macmillan, London.
Originally this work was published in *The English Illustrated Magazine*, April–September
1885, a periodical in which Crane published several poems. He also designed various
covers for it.

1887 *Four Winds Farm* by Mrs Molesworth.
Seven illustrations by Walter Crane, Macmillan, London.

Little Miss Peggy. Only a Nursery Story, by Mrs Molesworth.
Twelve illustrations by Walter Crane, Macmillan, London.

Legends for Lionel in pen and pencil
Text and colour illustrations by Walter Crane, Cassell, London.

Book Headings
A set of printer's headings designed for Messrs R. and R. Clark of Edinburgh.

Echoes of Hellas: The Tale of Troy and *The Story of Orestes*, from Homer and Aeschylus.
Introductory essays and sonnets by Professor George Warr.
82 red and black lithographed designs by Walter Crane, Marcus Ward, London.
A companion volume was issued as a pianoforte arrangement to the music of the stage
production, composed by Otto Goldschmidt, Malcolm Lawson, Walter Parratt and
Prof. W. H. Monk.

1888 *The Happy Prince and Other Tales*, by Oscar Wilde.
Three full-page illustrations by Walter Crane and decorative pieces by George J. A.
Combhood, David Nutt, London.

A Christmas Child: A Sketch of a Boy's Life by Mrs Molesworth.
Illustrations by Walter Crane, Macmillan, London.

A Christmas Posy by Mrs Molesworth.
Eight illustrations by Walter Crane, Macmillan, London.

1889 *Flora's Feast: A Masque of Flowers*
'Penned and Pictured' by Walter Crane with 40 colour plates, Cassell, London.
This book's popularity allowed Crane to follow it with other flower books such as *Queen
Summer*, 1891 and *A Floral Fantasy*, 1898 but *Flora's Feast* was the most successful.

The Rectory Children by Mrs Molesworth.
Seven illustrations by Walter Crane, Macmillan, London.

Walter Crane's Painting Book
A book of reprinted designs by Crane for children to colour, Routledge, London.

1890   *The Children of the Castle* by Mrs Molesworth.
Seven illustrations by Walter Crane, Macmillan, London.

The Turtle Dove's Nest and other Nursery Rhymes
Illustrations by Walter Crane and other artists, Routledge, London.

1891   *Renascence: A Book of Verse* by Walter Crane, with 39 line designs, reproduced by Walker and Leverett, Elkin Mathews, London.
This book contained *The Sirens Three* with other poems, although not in facsimile.

Queen Summer or The Tournament of the Rose
'Penned and Portrayed' by Walter Crane with 40 colour plates, Cassell, London.

The Triumph of Labour
A woodcut by Crane reproduced by Henry Sheu and published by Badoureau and Jones. Crane described this work as 'the largest and most important single design of mine in woodcut', commemorating Labour Day. Copies were made in Germany and the design was reissued in the folio *Cartoons for the Cause*, 1896. William Morris believed this design was the best work Crane had yet done.

1892   *The Claims of Decorative Art* by Walter Crane.
17 headpieces reproduced in red on white, white on red, by Walter Crane, Lawrence and Bullen, London.
The red and white colour scheme was similar to Crane's ceramic designs produced by Maw and Company. The book comprised essays for the revival of the arts of design and handicraft. German and Dutch editions were printed.

A Wonderbook for Boys and Girls by Nathaniel Hawthorne.
60 designs including 19 full-page colour plates by Walter Crane, Osgood and McIlvaine, London. These designs were completed while Crane lived in a small cottage in Florida; hence the appearance of tropical flora and fauna in the drawings.

The Tempest by William Shakespeare.
Eight designs by Walter Crane, engraved and printed by Duncan C. Dallas, J. M. Dent, London.

1893   *The Old Garden and Other Verses* by Margaret Deland.
Decorated throughout in colours by Walter Crane, Osgood and McIlvaine, London.

1894   *Two Gentlemen of Verona* by William Shakespeare.
Eight illustrations by Walter Crane, engraved and printed by Duncan C. Dallas, J. M. Dent, London (650 copies only).

The Story of the Glittering Plain or The Land of Living Men or The Acre of The Undying by William Morris.
23 illustrations by Walter Crane and decorative borders by Morris, engraved in wood by A. Leverett, Kelmscott Press. (The book was originally published without the Crane drawings, which Crane felt were not Gothic enough to suit Morris.)

The History of Reynard the Fox: with some account of his family, friends and associates
'A free rendering into verse of the translation made in the days of King Edward the Fourth by W. Caxton from the Dutch prose version of the story; with the addition of

some particular matters not therein set down but very needful to be known', by F. S. Ellis.
Photo-zincotype devices by Walter Crane, David Nutt, London (reissued in 1897).

The Faerie Queen by Edmund Spenser.
Edited by Thomas J. Wise, with full-page illustrations, tailpieces and initials by Walter Crane, George Allen, London.
The book was originally issued in nineteen parts, with individual wrappers also designed by Crane.

The Vision of Dante: A story for little children and a talk to their mothers by Elizabeth Harrison.
Illustrated with three plates by Walter Crane, The Chicago Kindergarten College, Chicago, U.S.A.

1896 *The Merry Wives of Windsor* by William Shakespeare.
Eight designs by Walter Crane, engraved and printed by Duncan C. Dallas, J. M. Dent, London.

Of the Decorative Illustration of Books Old and New by Walter Crane, Bell, London.
This book, designed entirely by Crane, is a survey of book illustration from the medieval to the contemporary. The final chapter deals with Crane's own theory of book design. Reprinted in 1973.

Cartoons for the Cause – A Souvenir of the International Socialist Workers and Trades Union Congress
Twelve full-page plates reproduced from drawings by Walter Crane from the socialist periodicals *Justice*, *The Commonweal*, and *The Clarion*, published between 1886 and 1896.

1898 *The Bases of Design* by Walter Crane, George Bell, London.
A series of lectures addressed to the students of the Manchester Municipal School of Art during the period when Crane was Director of Design.

The Shepheard's Calendar. 'Twelve Aeglogues proportionable to the twelve months. Entitled to the noble and virtuous gentlemen most worthy of all titles, both of Learning and Chivalry: Maister Philip Sidney' by Edmund Spenser with twelve illustrations and devices by Crane, Harper, London.

1899 *A Floral Fantasy in an Old English Garden* by Walter Crane.
46 full-page colour plates printed by Edmund Evans, Harper and Brothers, London. (Plates 5 and 46 are drawn from Crane's own figure.)

The Walter Crane Reader: First and Second Primers by Nellie Dale.
Title page and two full-page illustrations, many small drawings in colour by Walter Crane, J. M. Dent, London.

1900 *Line and Form* by Walter Crane, George Bell, London.
A student's guide to Crane's theories of decorative art, using his sketches and drawings for examples.

Don Quixote of La Mancha
Retold by Judge Parry with eleven full-page colour plates, and nineteen half-page black and white designs by Walter Crane, Blackie and Son, London.

1901   *A Masque of Days* from the *Last Essays of Elia*, by Charles Lamb.
Newly dressed and decorated by Walter Crane, with 40 colour plates and script design,
Cassell, London.

1903   *Moot Points*
Friendly disputes on Art and Industry between Walter Crane and Lewis F. Day, with
caricatures by Crane, B. T. Batsford, London.

1905   *A Flower Wedding described by Two Wallflowers* by Walter Crane.
40 full-page colour plates, Cassell, London.

1906   *The Children's Plutarch.*
Plutarch's *Lives* told in simple language by E. J. Gould, with six full-page illustrations
by Crane, Watts and Company, London.

Flowers from Shakespeare's Garden, A Posy from the Plays
Illustrated in 40 colour plates by Walter Crane, Cassell, London.

1907   *An Artist's Reminiscences* by Walter Crane.
123 illustrations by the author, Methuen, London.

The Dale Readers Book II by Nellie Dale.
Four full-page pictures and several colour and black and white drawings by Walter
Crane, George Philip, London.

1909   *The Rosebud and Other Tales* by Arthur Kelly.
Twenty full-page colour illustrations by Walter Crane, T. Fisher Unwin, London.

1911   *King Arthur's Knights: The Tales Retold for Boys and Girls* by Henry Gilbert.
Sixteen full-page colour plates by Walter Crane, T. C. and E. C. Jack, Edinburgh.

William Morris to Whistler: Papers and Addresses on Art and Crafts and the Commonweal.
Illustrations by Walter Crane, George Bell, London.

1912   *Robin Hood and the Men of the Greenwood* by Henry Gilbert.
Sixteen full-page colour illustrations by Walter Crane, T. C. and E. C. Jack, Edinburgh.

1913   *The Story of Greece told to Boys and Girls* by Mary MacGregor.
Nineteen colour plates by Walter Crane, T. C. and E. C. Jack, Edinburgh.

1915   *The Knights of the Round Table* by Henry Gilbert.
Eight illustrations in colour by Walter Crane, T. C. and E. C. Jack, Edinburgh.

Robin Hood and His Merry Men by Henry Gilbert.
Eight illustrations in colour by Walter Crane, T. C. and E. C. Jack, Edinburgh.

The following chronological list of books and articles are valuable references for the art and life of Walter Crane or his contemporaries.

Crane, Lucy. *Art and the Formation of Taste*, with illustrations by T. and Walter Crane, 1882.

Stephens, F. G. Review, *The Portfolio*, January, 1890, pp. 12–19.

Mr. Crane and his Picturebooks, *Pall Mall Budget*, 5 June 1891, pp. 6–7.

Catalogue of a Collection of Designs by Walter Crane with prefatory explanatory notes by the artist. *Fine Art Society Catalogue No. 89*, London, 1891.

Catalogue of a Collection of Designs by Walter Crane, Nicholson Institute, Leek, 1892.

Crane, Walter. The English Revival of Decorative Art, *Fortnightly Review*, 1892.

Artist's letter, *The Daily Chronicle*, 4 February 1893.

Day, Lewis. A Kensington Interior (Ionides), *Art Journal* (London), Vol. 55, 1893, pp. 133–44.

Naar Walter Crane's *Claims of Decorative Art*, in het Nederlandsch bewerkt door Jan Veth, en verrierd met talrijke Vignetten in hout gesneden door G. W. Dijsselhof, *Kunst en samen leving*, Vol. IX, p. 171, Amsterdam, 1894.

Review, *The Daily Chronicle*, 26 March 1895.

Crane, Walter. William Morris, *Scribner's Magazine*, XXII, 1897, p. 88.

Crane, Walter. *The Work of Walter Crane* with notes by the artist, *Art Annual*, Vol. 17, 1898.

Konody, Paul C. *The Art of Walter Crane*, George Bell, London, 1902.

Schleinitz, Otto von. *Walter Crane*, Berlin, 1902.

Hardie, Martin. *English Coloured Books*, Methuen, London, 1906.

Crane, Beatrice. *The Procession of the Months*. The verses of B. Crane with designs by W. Crane, 1908.

Brown, Frank P. *South Kensington and its Art Training* with a foreword by Walter Crane, Longmans and Green, London, 1912.

Catalogue, *Illustration et décoration du livre*, British Arts and Crafts Exhibition, 1914.

Masse, Gertrude. *Bibliography of First Editions of Books illustrated by Walter Crane*. Preface by Heyward Sumner, frontispiece portrait by G. F. Watts, Chelsea, London, 1923.

Walter Crane Hazelford Sketchbook. A sampler with autobiographical notes, John Barnard Associates, Cambridge, Massachusetts, 1937.

Mahony, Bertha.   *Illustrators of Children's Books 1744–1945*, Horn Books, Boston, 1947.

Laski, Marghanita.   *Mrs Ewing, Mrs Molesworth, Mrs Hodgson Burnett*, Arthur Barker, London, 1950.

Mathews, Brander.   *Bookbindings Old and New*, George Bell, London, n.d.

MacLean, Ruari.   *Reminiscences of Edmund Evans*, Oxford University Press, Oxford, 1967.

Tailpiece from *Grimm's Household Stories*, 1882